Wishing well, wishing well,
what can I get,

If I make a wish
with my fishing net?

I can wish for a ride
on a jumbo jet.

I can wish for a car
and a big gold bar.

I can wish for a big train set.

I can fly as far
as a silver star.

I can wish for a funny pet.

I can play the guitar
like a big pop-star.

I can wish ... for a fishing net!

I can catch some tadpoles.
They don't swim far.

I'll take them home
in a big jam jar.

That's what I'll get
with my fishing net.